W9-AZI-471

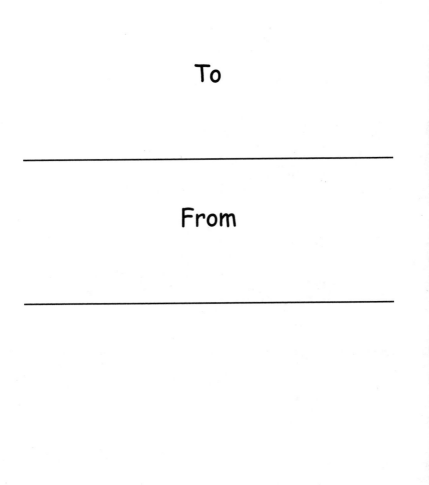

To

_____

From

Little Book

DEVOTIONS

31 DAILY DEVOTIONALS

Honesty

Little Book
DEVOTIONS

Honesty

ISBN 1-58334-189-7

The quoted ideas expressed in this book (but not scripture verses) are not, in all cases, exact quotations, as some have been edited for clarity and brevity. In all cases, the author has attempted to maintain the speaker's original intent. In some cases, quoted material for this book was obtained from secondary sources, primarily print media. While every effort was made to ensure the accuracy of these sources, the accuracy cannot be guaranteed. For additions, deletions, corrections or clarifications in future editions of this text, please write BIRGHTON BOOKS.

Scripture taken from the HOLY BIBLE, NEW INTERNATIONAL VERSION ©. NIV ©. Copyright © 1973, 1978, 1984, by International Bible Society. Used by permission of Zondervan Publishing House. All rights reserved.

Scripture quoted from the *International Children's Bible®, New Century Version®*, copyright © 1986,1988,1999 by Tommy Nelson™, a division of Thomas Nelson, Inc. Nashville, Tennessee 37214. Used by permission.

Scripture quotations marked (TLB) are taken from The Holy Bible, The Living Bible Translation, Copyright © 1971. Used by permission of Tyndale House Publishers, Incorporated, Wheaton, Illinois 60189. All rights reserved.

Scripture quotations marked (NLT) are taken from The Holy Bible, New Living Translation, Copyright © 1996. Used by permission of Tyndale House Publishers, Incorporated, Wheaton, Illinois 60189. All rights reserved.

Scripture taken from the NEW AMERICAN STANDARD BIBLE®, Copyright © 1960, 1962, 1963, 1968, 1971, 1972, 1973, 1975, 1977, 1995 by The Lockman Foundation. Used by permission.

Printed in the United States of America
Cover Design: Kim Russel, Wahoo Designs
Page Layout: Bart Dawson

1 2 3 4 5 6 7 8 9 10 • 02 03 04 05 06 07 08 09 10

For All of God's Children

Table of Contents

A Message to Parents

Perhaps your child's library is already overflowing with brightly colored children's books. If so, congratulations: you're a thoughtful parent who understands the importance of reading to young children.

This little book is an important addition to your child's library. It is intended to be read *by* Christian parents *to* their young children. The text contains 31 brief chapters, one for each day of the month. Each chapter contains a Bible verse, a brief story or lesson, tips for kids and parents, and a prayer. Every chapter examines a different aspect of an important Biblical theme: honesty.

For the next 31 days, try this experiment: read one chapter each night to your child, and then spend a few more moments talking about the chapter's meaning. By the end of the month, you will have had 31 different opportunities to share God's wisdom with your son or daughter, and that's a very good thing.

If you have been touched by God's love and His grace, then you know the joy that He has brought into your own life. Now it's your turn to share His message with the boy or girl whom He has entrusted to your care. Happy reading! And may God richly bless you and your family now and forever.

Tell the Truth

1

Good people will be guided by honesty.

✿ ✿ ✿

Proverbs 11:3 ICB

Maybe you've heard this phrase: "Honesty is the best policy." And, of course, it is *the best* policy, but more importantly, it is also *God's* policy.

If we want to please God, we must honor Him by obeying His commandments. He has commanded us to be honest with everybody. Truth is God's way, and it must be our way, too.

If you're not sure that it's the right thing to do, don't do it! And if you're not sure that it's the truth, don't tell it.

WOW

Don't worry about what you do not understand. Worry about what you do understand in the Bible but do not live by.

Corrie ten Boom

And the greatest example is . . . you! Your children will learn about life from many sources; the most important source can and should be you. But remember that the lectures you *give* are never as important as the ones you *live*.

Dear Lord,
help me be a person whose words
are true and whose heart is pure.
In everything that I do, let me
use Jesus as my model and my
guide, today and always.

Amen

It's Up to You!

Lord, teach me what you want me to do.
And I will live by your truth.

❖ ❖ ❖

Psalm 86:11 ICB

Nobody can tell the truth for you. You're the one who decides what you are going to say. You're the one who decides whether your words will be truthful . . . or not.

The word "integrity" means doing the right and honest thing. If you're going to be a person of integrity, it's up to you. If you want to live a life that is pleasing to God *and* to others, make integrity a habit. When you do, everybody wins, *especially* you!

Don't play the blame game: it's very tempting to blame others when you make mistakes or say something that isn't true. But it's more honest to look in the mirror first.

WOW

We must constantly strive to keep our integrity intact. When wealth is lost, nothing is lost; when health is lost, something is lost; when character is lost, all is lost.

Billy Graham

Family values? Family priorities! Hopefully, your family's value system is built on the Rock that cannot be moved. As a parent, you must help your children understand that God is the priority that never comes "next."

Dear Lord,
teach me to be a truthful, kind,
generous person every day that
I live. Let me live by Your rules,
and let me accept the love of
Your Son, now and forever.

Amen

Doing the Right Thing

Doing what is right brings freedom
to honest people.

❈ ❈ ❈

Proverbs 11:6 ICB

Doing the right thing isn't always easy, especially when we're tired or frustrated. But, doing the *wrong* thing almost always leads to trouble. And sometimes, it leads to BIG trouble.

When you do the right thing, you don't have to worry about what you did or what you said. But, if you are dishonest—or if you do something that you know is wrong—you'll be worried that someone will find out. So do the right thing; it may be harder in the beginning, but it's easier in the end.

KiD TiP

If you're not sure what to do . . . ask yourself this question: "Would I be embarrassed if somebody found out?" If the answer is "Yes," don't do it!

WOW

Hate what is evil. Hold on to what is good.
Romans 12:9 ICB

Teaching takes time: Helping our children understand the fundamental truths of Christian living requires time, and lots of it. Our children are always learning. As parents, we must ensure that they are learning *from us.*

Dear Lord,
let me do the right thing today
and every day. Let me treat
other people with honesty and
respect. And, let the things that
I say and do show my family and
friends that I love them . . .
and that I love You.

Amen

Little Lies Grow Into Big Ones!

The honest person will live safely, but
the one who is dishonest will be caught.

❀ ❀ ❀

Proverbs 10:9 ICB

Sometimes, people can convince themselves that it's okay to tell "little white lies." And, sometimes people convince themselves that itsy bitsy lies aren't harmful. But there's a problem: little lies have a way of growing into big ones, and once they grow up, they cause lots of problems.

Remember that lies, no matter what size, are not part of God's plan for our lives, so tell the truth about everything. It's the right thing to do, and besides: when you always tell the truth, you don't have to try to remember what you said!

It's better to say nothing: If you're tempted to say something that isn't true, don't say anything. A closed mouth tells no lies.

WOW

Fill the heart with the love of Christ
so that only truth and purity can
come out of the mouth.

Warren Wiersbe

White lies are better left untold: If we hedge the truth, so will they.

Dear Lord,
let me tell the truth about big
things *and* about little things.
Help me remember that little
lies can sometimes be as hurtful
as big ones. So, instead of
worrying about *how much* truth
to tell, let me speak *only* true
words, today and every day.

Amen

The Bible Says . . .

Your word is like a lamp for my feet
and a light for my way.

❀ ❀ ❀

Psalm 119:105 ICB

What book contains everything that God has to say about honesty? The Bible, of course. If you read the Bible every day, you'll soon be convinced that honesty is *very* important to God. And, since honesty is important to God, it should be important to you, too.

The Bible is the most important book you'll ever own. It's God's Holy Word. Read it every day, and follow its instructions. If you do, you'll be safe now and forever.

Who's supposed to be taking care of your Bible? If it's you, then take *very* good care of it; it's by far the most important book you own!

WOW

The Bible is like no other book.
Treat it that way!

Marie T. Freeman

Children's Bible? Strongly consider it! If your child doesn't already own one, consider purchasing a translation of the Holy Bible specifically intended for children. These translations are amazingly helpful because of their simplicity and clarity.

Dear Lord,
You have given me a wonderful
gift: the Holy Bible. Let me
read it and understand it
and follow the commandments
that I find there.

Amen

When Telling the Truth is Hard

6

I asked the Lord for help, and
he answered me. He saved me
from all that I feared.

❖ ❖ ❖

Psalm 34:4 ICB

Telling the truth can be hard sometimes. But even when telling the truth is *very* hard, that's exactly what you should do. If you're afraid to tell the truth, pray to God for the courage to do the right thing, and then do it!

If you've ever told a big lie, and then had to live with the big consequences of that lie, you know that it's far more trouble to tell a lie than it is to tell the truth. But lies aren't just troubling to us; they're also troubling to God! So tell the truth, even when it's hard to do; you'll be glad you did . . . and so will He!

KiD TiP

When it's hard to tell the truth: When telling the truth is hard, that probably means that you're afraid of what others might think—or what they might do—when you're truthful. Remember that it is usually better to face those kinds of problems *now* rather than *later!*

WOW
Make all your decisions in the light of Jesus Christ.
Oswald Chambers

Parent Tip

When the truth is hard for parents: telling the truth isn't just hard for kids; it can be hard for parents, too. And when honesty is hard, that's precisely the moment when wise parents remember that their children are watching . . . and learning.

Dear Lord,
let me tell the truth, even when
telling the truth is hard.
Give me the courage and
the wisdom to be honest with
my family and with my friends,
today and every day.

Amen

7

Solomon Says

Keep your eyes focused on what is right.
Keep looking straight ahead
to what is good.

✸ ✸ ✸

Proverbs 4:25 ICB

In the Book of Proverbs, King Solomon gave us wonderful advice for living wisely. Solomon said that we should keep our eyes "focused on what is right." In other words, we should do our best to say and do the things that we know are pleasing to God.

The next time you're tempted to say an unkind word or to say something that isn't true, remember the advice of King Solomon. Solomon said that it's always better to do the right thing, even when it's tempting to do otherwise.

So if you know something is wrong, don't do it; instead, do what you know to be right. When you do, you'll be saving yourself a lot of trouble and you'll be obeying the Word of God.

KiD TiP

Simon says? Solomon says! Have you ever played the game Simon Says? When you play it, you're not supposed to move until the leader calls out, "Simon Says!" Wise King Solomon had many rules for living. You should get to know those rules—especially the ones found in the Book of Proverbs. Then, you can be guided by the things that *Solomon says!*

WOW

To obey God means to belong to God, and to belong to God means to have all His infinite power. To belong to God means to have all.
Hannah Whitall Smith

Parent Tip

Get to know the Book of Proverbs: and help your child get to know it, too (a children's translation of the Bible can help!).

Dear Lord,
let me grow up to become wise.
Let me study Your Word and
learn Your ways so that I can
become the kind of Christian
that You want me to be.

Amen

Saying Bad Things About Other People

A person who gossips ruins friendships.
❈ ❈ ❈
Proverbs 16:28 ICB

Do you know what gossip is? It's when we say bad things about people who are not around to hear us. When we say bad things about other people, we hurt them *and* we hurt ourselves. That's why the Bible tells us that gossip is wrong.

When we say things that we don't want other people to know we said, we're being *somewhat* dishonest, but if the things we say *aren't true*, we're being *very* dishonest. Either way, we have done something that we will regret later, especially if the other person finds out.

So do yourself a big favor: don't gossip. It's a waste of words, and it's the wrong thing to do. You'll feel better about yourself if you don't gossip about other people. So don't do it!

Don't say something behind someone's back that you wouldn't say to that person's face.

WOW
The things you say in the dark will be told in the light. The things you have whispered in an inner room will be shouted from the top of the house.

Luke 12:3 ICB

Make your home a safe haven from gossip: Gossip is a learned behavior. Make certain that your children don't learn it *from you!*

Dear Lord,
make me a person who says the
same things *to* other people that
I say *about* them. Make my
words helpful, encouraging, and
true. And let the light of Christ
shine in me and through me,
today and forever.

Amen

Honesty and the Golden Rule

9

Do for other people the same things
you want them to do for you.

❁ ❁ ❁

Matthew 7:12 ICB

Do you want other people to be honest with you? Of course you do. And that's why you should be honest with them. The words of Matthew 7:12 remind us that, as believers in Christ, we should treat others as we wish to be treated. And that means telling them the truth!

The Golden Rule is your tool for deciding how you will treat other people. When you use the Golden Rule as your guide for living, your words and your actions will be pleasing to other people *and* to God.

Use the Golden Rule to help you decide what to say: If you wouldn't like something said about *you*, then you probably shouldn't say it about *somebody else!*

WOW

Do all the good you can. By all the means you can. In all the ways you can.
In all the places you can. At all the times you can. To all the people you can.
As long as you can.

John Wesley

The Rule in action! When you live according to the principle of the Golden Rule, your children will notice, and the results will be as good as gold . . . make that *better* than gold!

Dear Lord,
let me be honest with other
people in the same way that
I want them to be honest with
me. Let me keep the Golden Rule
today and every day, Lord,
so that I will become the kind
of person that Jesus
wants me to be.

Amen

10

Honesty Starts at Home

He blesses the home of the righteous.

❀ ❀ ❀

Proverbs 3:33 NIV

Should you be honest with your parents? Certainly. With your brothers and sisters? Of course. With cousins, grandparents, aunts, and uncles? Yes! In fact, you should be honest with *everybody* in your family because honesty starts at home.

If you can't be honest in your own house, how can you expect to be honest in other places, like at church or at school? So make sure that you're completely honest with your family. If you are, then you're much more likely to be honest with everybody else.

Since you love your family . . . let them know it by the things you say and the things you do. And, never take your family members for granted; they deserve your very best treatment!

WOW

A Christian home is the Carpenter's workshop. It is the place where the Carpenter from Galilee builds lives for today and for eternity.

Criswell Freeman

Make Christ the cornerstone: Every family is built upon a foundation; let yours be the love of God and the salvation of Christ.

Dear Lord,
You have given me a family that
cares for me and loves me. Let
me treat all my family members
with honesty, kindness, love,
and respect. Always!

Amen

11

God is
Watching!

I am the Lord, and I can look into
a person's heart.

✵ ✵ ✵

Jeremiah 17:10 ICB

Even when you think nobody is watching, God is. Nothing that we say or do escapes the watchful eye of our Lord. God understands that we are not perfect, but He also wants us to live according to *His* rules, not *our own.*

The next time that you're tempted to say something that you shouldn't say or to do something that you shouldn't do, remember that you can't keep secrets from God. So don't even try!

Made a mistake? Ask for forgiveness? If you've broken one of God's rules, you can always ask Him for His forgiveness. And He will always give it!

WOW

You can see God from anywhere. And He can see *you* from anywhere.

A. W. Tozer

He's watching us, too. Of course we know that God watches over us, but we must also make certain that our children *know that we know*. And, we must behave in ways that let our children know that *we* know that *He* knows. Whew!

Dear Lord,
thank You for watching over me.
Let the things that I say and do
be pleasing to You. And Lord,
thank You for Your love;
let me share it with others
today and every day.

Amen

12

An Honest Friend . . .

Tell each other the truth because we all belong to each other . . . .

❃ ❃ ❃

Ephesians 4:25 ICB

All genuine friendships are built upon both honesty and trust. Without trust, friends soon drift apart. But with trust, friends can stay friends for a lifetime.

As Christians, we should always try to be trustworthy, encouraging, loyal friends. And, we should be thankful for the people who are loyal friends to us. When we treat other people with honesty and respect, we not only make more friends, but we also keep the friendships we've already made.

Do you want friends *you* can trust? Then start by being a friend *they* can trust. That's the way to make *your* friendships strong, stronger, and strongest!

Lies tear down trust: one of the very best ways to destroy a friendship is to lie to your friend . . . so don't do it!

WOW
It is the duty of every Christian to be Christ to his neighbor.
Martin Luther

Trust starts at the top: In every family, trust starts with the older generation and works its way down to the younger ones. We must teach our children how to be trust-worthy by *being* trustworthy. There simply is no other way.

Dear Lord,
help me to be an honest friend.
Since I want other people
to be truthful with me,
let me be truthful with them,
today and every day.

Amen

13
Listen to Your Conscience

So I strive always to keep my conscience
clear before God and man.

❁ ❁ ❁

Acts 24:16 NIV

Sometimes, you know that something isn't the right thing to do, but you do it anyway. Even if no one else knows, you know . . . and so does God! You can keep secrets from other people, but you can't keep secrets from Him. God knows what you think and what you do.

If your heart tells you not to do something, don't do it! If your conscience tells you that something is wrong, stop! If you're tempted to say something that isn't true, don't! You can keep secrets from other people some of the time, but God is watching all of the time, and He sees everything, including your heart.

That tiny little voice inside your head . . .
is called your conscience. Treat it like a
trusted friend: Listen to the things it says;
it's usually right!

WOW

One's conscience can only be satisfied
when God is satisfied.

C. H. Spurgeon

**Sometimes, the little voice that we hear
in our heads can be the echoes of our own
parents' voices** . . . and now that we're parents ourselves, we're the ones whose words
will echo down through the hearts and minds
of future generations. It's a big responsi-
bility, but with God's help, we're up to the
challenge.

Dear Lord,
other people see me only from
the outside, but You know my
heart. Let my heart be pure,
and let me listen to the voice
that You have placed there,
today and every day that I live.

Amen

14

Honesty at School

Being respected is more important
than having great riches.
✿ ✿ ✿
Proverbs 22:1 ICB

If you are going to school, you already know that it's important to tell the truth when you are in the classroom. And, you know that it's not right to take things that are not yours.

Of course, some children will behave *dishonestly*, and soon everyone will know what they have done. Other children will behave *honestly*, and soon everyone will know that the honest kids can be trusted.

What kind of student do you want to be? Do you want to be a person who is respected, or not? Do you want to be a person who is trusted, or not? The choice is yours, and the choice should be obvious.

Put it back! If, in a moment of weakness, you took something that isn't yours, put it back . . . now!

WOW
If I take care of my character,
my reputation will take care of itself.

D. L. Moody

Honesty at school starts at home: don't expect teachers to teach the lessons that parents should have already taught!

Dear Lord,
You have given me rules to live
by. Help me to obey those
rules in every situation so that
wherever I happen to be,
my words and my actions
will be pleasing to You.

Amen

15

When We're Dishonest . . .

Dishonesty will destroy those who
are not trustworthy.

❋ ❋ ❋

Proverbs 11:3 ICB

Have you ever said something that wasn't true? When you did, were you sorry for what you had said? Probably so.

When we're dishonest, we make ourselves unhappy in surprising ways. Here are just a few troubles that result from dishonesty: we feel guilty *and* we are usually found out *and* we disappoint others *and* we disappoint God. It's easy to see that lies always cause more problems than they solve.

Happiness and honesty always go hand in hand. But it's up to you to make sure that *you* go hand in hand with them!

KID TIP

Did you tell a lie? Apologize and make it right! Did you say something that was untrue? Then it's time to make things right by telling the truth. It's never too late to tell the truth, but it's never too early, either!

WOW

Then Jesus said, "So I also don't judge you. You may go now, but don't sin again."

John 8:11 ICB

Parent Tip

When kids are dishonest: Face it: even the most angelic children can say things that are untrue. When we observe such behavior in *our own* children, we must be understanding, but firm. We live in a world where dishonesty is too often tolerated. But inside the walls of our own homes, dishonesty should never be ignored; it should be corrected by loving, courageous parents.

PRAY TIME

Dear Lord,
when I make mistakes, help me
to correct them. And then, Lord,
help me to not make those same
mistakes again. Let me become
wiser each day so that I can
become the kind of Christian
that You want me to be.

Amen

16

Honesty and Kindness

Don't ever stop being kind and truthful.
Let kindness and truth show in all you do.

✸ ✸ ✸

Proverbs 3:3 ICB

Honesty and kindness should go hand in hand. In other words, we shouldn't use honesty as an excuse to hurt other people's feelings.

It's easy to find faults in other people, and easy to tease other people about their shortcomings. But it's wrong. When we needlessly hurt other people's feelings, we are disobeying God.

The Bible tells us that we should never stop being kind *and* truthful. And, that's very good advice for caring, thoughtful Christians . . . like you!

Don't be cruel: Sometimes, you can be *too* honest, especially if you say unkind things that are intended to hurt other people's feelings. When you're deciding what to say, you should mix honesty *and* courtesy. When you do, you'll say the right thing.

WOW
The great test of a person's
character is his speech.
Oswald Chambers

Avoid Cynicism, Spread Optimism: We live in a world that often resembles a desert of cynicism and mistrust. Therefore, we must make our homes oases of optimism and faith.

Dear Lord,
help me to be a person who
is both honest and kind.
Let my words be truthful *and*
encouraging. Let me always
remember the Golden Rule, and
let me speak accordingly.

Amen

17

Crying "Wolf!"

Innocent people will be kept safe.
But those who are dishonest
will suddenly be ruined.

❈ ❈ ❈

Proverbs 28:18 ICB

Perhaps you've heard the story of the boy who cried "wolf!" In that story, the boy exaggerated his problems and eventually got himself into BIG trouble!

When we pretend that our troubles are worse than they really are, we may earn a little sympathy now, but we'll invite lots of trouble later.

If you're ever tempted to cry "wolf!," don't. Exaggeration wasn't good for the boy who cried "wolf!," and it's not good for you.

Don't Exaggerate! All of us have enough troubles without pretending that we have more.

WOW

Character is what you are in the dark.

D. L. Moody

Don't Exaggerate, Part II: If you tend to overestimate your problems and undercount your blessings, your kids will, too. But if you assess your problems realistically and seek the Lord's help in solving them, your children will learn that no problem is too big for God.

Dear Lord,
let me always remember that
none of my problems are ever
too big for You!

Amen

18

It's Easier to Tell the Truth

The goodness of an innocent person
makes his life easier.

❀ ❀ ❀

Proverbs 11:5 ICB

Sometimes, telling the truth is hard to do, but even then, it's easier to tell the truth than it is to live with the consequences of telling a lie. You see, telling a lie can be easier in the beginning, but it's always harder in the end! In the end, when people find out that you've been untruthful, they may feel hurt and you will feel embarrassed.

So make this promise to yourself, and keep it: don't let lies rob you of your happiness. Instead, tell the truth from the start. You'll be doing yourself a big favor, and you'll be obeying the Word of God.

KiD TiP

If a little lie gets started, nip it in the bud: it's always easier to stop a tiny lie before it has had a chance to grow up into a very big lie! Telling the truth stops the lie from growing.

WOW
Honesty has a beautiful and refreshing simplicity about it.
Chuck Swindoll

Discuss the importance of integrity: Teach the importance of integrity every day, and, if necessary, use words.

Dear Lord,
let me be honest about big things
and about little things. When I
tell the truth, my life is better
and my conscience is clear, so let
me tell the truth *and* live it,
today and every day.

Amen

19

When We Make Mistakes

But if we confess our sins, he will forgive
our sins. We can trust God. He does what
is right. He will make us clean from all
the wrongs that we have done.

❀ ❀ ❀

1 John 1:9 ICB

Do you make mistakes? We all do. Nobody is perfect, and you should not expect to be perfect, either.

When you make a mistake, the best thing to do is to admit it, to correct it, and to try very hard not to make it again. Then, your mistakes can become opportunities to learn.

Sometimes, mistakes can be the very best way to learn, so learn from them. But don't keep making the same mistake over and over again. That's not learning; that's silly!

Fix it sooner rather than later: If you make a mistake or say something that isn't true, the time to make things better is now, not later! The sooner you admit your mistake, the better.

WOW

To make a mistake is human, but to remain in error is wrong.

Saint Augustine

Be Consistent: Of course there will be times when you feel anger toward your children, but your love for them should never be in question. Parental love must never be turned on and off like the garden hose; it should, instead, flow like a mighty river, too deep to touch bottom and too strong to stop.

Dear Lord,
when I make mistakes, let me
admit them and correct them.
When I am wrong, let me be
quick to change and quick to ask
forgiveness from others
and from You.

Amen

It's a Habit!

We must not become tired of doing good.

❈ ❈ ❈

Galatians 6:2 ICB

Our lives are made up of lots and lots of habits. And the habits we choose help determine the kind of people we become. If we choose habits that are good, we are happier and healthier. If we choose habits that are bad, then it's too bad for us!

Honesty, like so many other things, is a habit. And it's a habit that is right for you.

Do you want to grow up to become the kind of person that God intends for you to be? Then get into the habit of being honest with everybody. You'll be glad you did . . . and so will God!

Choose all your habits carefully: habits are easier to make than they are to break, so be careful!

WOW
Since behaviors become habits,
make them work with you
and not against you.
E. Stanley Jones

Make Encouragement a Habit: Deliberately look for ways to encourage and praise your children . . . every day. Good deeds and good words can become habit-forming.

Dear Lord,
help me to be an honest person
all the time, not just *some of the
time*. And let the things that
I say and do be pleasing to You
this day and every day.

Amen

21

Growing Up with God

He will teach us of his ways,
and we will walk in his paths.

✸ ✸ ✸

Isaiah 2:3 KJV

When will you stop growing up? With any luck, never! If you keep studying God's Word and obeying His commandments, you will never be a "fully grown" Christian. You will always be a "growing" Christian.

An important part of growing up is learning that honesty is better than dishonesty and that true words are better than lies. You have already learned that lesson; now, it's time to put your knowledge to good use by doing the things that you know are right.

God knows you can't be perfect, but He doesn't want you to keep doing bad things, either! Instead, God wants you to keep growing in the love and knowledge of His Son. When you do, you'll keep on growing, and that's exactly the kind of Christian that God wants you to become.

Daily Devotionals? Yes! Try your best to read the Bible with your parents every day. If they forget, remind them!

WOW
A Christian is never in a state
of completion but always in
the process of becoming.
Martin Luther

Making time for God: Our days are filled to the brim with obligations and priorities, but no priority is greater than our obligation to our Creator. Let's make sure that we give Him the time He deserves, not only on Sundays, but also on every other day of the week.

Dear Lord,
let me always keep learning about
Your love and about Your Son,
Jesus. Make me a better person
today than I was yesterday, and
let me continue to grow as a
Christian every day that I live.

Amen

22

Tell the Truth
and
Don't Worry!

It is better to be poor and honest than
to be foolish and tell lies.

❁ ❁ ❁

Proverbs 19:1 ICB

When we tell a lie, the trouble starts. Lots of trouble. But when we tell the truth—and nothing but the truth—we stop Old Man Trouble in his tracks.

When we always tell the truth, we make our worries smaller, not bigger. And that's precisely what God wants us to do.

So, if you would like to have fewer worries and more happiness, abide by this simple rule: tell the truth, the whole truth, and nothing but the truth. When you do, you'll make many of your worries disappear altogether. And that's the truth!

Worried about something you said or did?
If you made a mistake yesterday, the day to fix it is today. Then, you won't have to worry about it tomorrow.

WOW
Pray, and let God worry.
Martin Luther

Problem solving 101: Your children will learn how to solve their problems by observing you. So remember: when it comes to solving problems, it's better to invest more time *working on them* and less time *fretting over them*.

Dear Lord,
if I make a mistake,
let me correct it. If I say
something that is untrue,
let me apologize. If I behave
badly, let me correct my bad
behavior. Let me do the best
I can, Lord, and then let me
leave the worrying up to You.

Amen

23

Sooner or Later, the Truth Comes Out!

Everything that is hidden will be shown.
Everything that is secret will be
made known.

✦ ✦ ✦

Luke 12:2 ICB

How often do lies stay hidden? Not very often. Usually, the truth has a way of coming out, and usually it comes out sooner rather than later. That's one of the reasons that it's so silly to tell lies: lying simply doesn't work!

Truth, on the other hand, works extremely well. When you tell the truth, you don't have to remember what you said, and there's nothing bad for other people to find out. So do yourself a favor and get into the habit of telling the truth about *everything*. Otherwise, you'll be letting yourself in for a whole lot of trouble, and you'll be letting yourself in for it *soon!*

You've got a secret? Probably not! Keeping lies hidden is usually impossible, so why even try?

WOW
Lying covers a multitude of sins—
temporarily.
D. L. Moody

A family secret is a contradiction in terms. Most family secrets aren't. So why even try?

Dear Lord,
sooner or later, the truth has a
way of coming out. So give me
the wisdom and the courage
to tell the truth in the very
beginning. The truth is Your way,
Lord; let be it my way, too.

Amen

How Truthful is the Truth?

Then you will know the truth,
and the truth will set you free.

❀ ❀ ❀

John 8:32 NIV

Jesus had a message for all of His followers. He said, "The truth will set you free." When we do the right thing and tell the truth, we don't need to worry about our lies catching up with us. When we behave honestly, we don't have to worry about feeling guilty or ashamed. But, if we fail to do what we know is right, bad things start to happen, and we feel guilty.

Jesus understood that the truth is a very good thing indeed. We should understand it, too. And, we should keep telling it as long as we live.

The Truth with a capital "T": Jesus is the Truth with a capital "T" . . . and that's the truth!

WOW

The Spirit of God brings to our minds the need for truth.

C. H. Spurgeon

Parent Tip

The Truth with a capital "T," Part II: Hannah Whitall Smith wrote, "The crucial question for each of us is this: What do you think of Jesus, and do you yet have a personal acquaintance with Him?" As parents, we must also ask ourselves another question: do our children know what we think about Jesus? And *if* not, *why* not?

Dear Lord,
thank You for Your Son Jesus.
Let Him be the light of my life,
the Savior of my soul, and the
model for my behavior.

Amen

How Would Jesus Behave?

So Jesus said to the Jews who believed in him, "If you continue to obey my teaching, you are truly my followers.

❁ ❁ ❁

John 8:31 ICB

If you are tempted to say something that isn't true, stop and ask yourself a simple question: "How would Jesus behave if He were here?" The answer to that question will tell you what to say.

Jesus told His followers that the truth would make them free. As believers, we must do our best to know the truth *and* to tell it. When we do, we behave as our Savior behaved, and that's exactly how God wants us to behave.

KiD TiP

Learn from your Bible: Start learning about Jesus, and keep learning about Him as long as you live. His story never grows old, and His teachings never fail.

WOW
Tell me the story of Jesus.
Write on my heart every word.
Tell me the story most precious,
sweetest that ever was heard.
Fanny Crosby

Parent Tip

Hymnal alert! Every home should have several well-used hymnals. After all, few things in life are better than a family sing-along, even if Granddad sings a little off key.

Dear Lord,
the Bible is Your gift to me.
Let me use it, let me trust it,
and let me obey it, today
and every day that I live.

Amen

That Belongs to Someone Else!

You must not steal.

❀ ❀ ❀

Exodus 20:15 ICB

Have you ever been tempted to take something that didn't belong to you? If you did steal, you probably felt bad about doing so, and with good reason. We all know that it's wrong to take things that don't belong to us, but sometimes we do it anyway. Why? Because we aren't strong enough or smart enough not to.

God's plan for your life does not include stealing, so don't do it. Ever.

If it belongs to somebody else, don't take it. Don't even *think* about taking it! Don't even *think about thinking about taking it*. Don't even *think about thinking about thinking about* . . . oh well, you get the point!

Want something? Ask, don't take! It's okay to ask. It's *not* okay to take!

WOW

Many jokes are made about the devil,
but the devil is no joke. He is called
a deceiver. Two forces are at work in our
world—the forces of Christ and
the forces of the devil—and you are
asked to choose.

Billy Graham

When angels fall . . . Even your own angelic child may make a mistake on occasion. When the unlikely happens, help your boy or girl understand *why* the behavior is wrong and *how* to prevent it in the future.

Dear Lord,
help me to turn away from
dishonesty so that I can live in
the comfort of Your truth,
now and forever.

Amen

27
God's Way is Always Best

The thing you should want most is God's kingdom and doing what God wants. Then all these other things you need will be given to you.

✸ ✸ ✸

Matthew 6:33 ICB

In life, you always have choices. You decide whether you'll be honest, or not. You decide whether you'll behave wisely, or not. You decide whether you'll obey God, or not.

The choices you make help determine whether you are happy or sad. They also determine what kind of person you will become.

It's never too early to begin making good choices. And, if you're old enough to understand these words, then the time for you to start making good choices is NOW!

KiD TiP

Too many choices? If you're faced with too many questions and too few answers, turn your concerns over to God in prayer. When you do, you'll discover that He has more answers than you have questions.

WOW

Life is a series of choices between
the bad, the good, and the best.
Everything depends on how we choose.

Vance Havner

Parent Tip

Some choices WE must make: of course we want to give our children room to grow, but some decisions must be reserved for the wisest men and women of the family (us). Those choices include matters of personal health and safety *and* the core principles by which we, as parents, intend to raise our families.

Dear Lord,
help me to make choices that
are pleasing to You. Help me
to be honest, patient, and kind.
And above all, help me to follow
the teachings of Jesus, not just
today, but every day.

Amen

Need Help? Ask God!

Continue to ask, and God will give to you.
Continue to search and you will find.
Continue to knock, and the door
will open for you.

✦ ✦ ✦

Matthew 7:7 ICB

Perhaps you've tried to be more honest with other people, but you're still falling back into your old habits. If so, don't get discouraged. Instead, become even more determined to become the person God wants you to be.

If you trust God, and if you keep asking Him to help you become a more truthful person, He will help you make yourself into that person. So, if at first you don't succeed, keep praying. God is listening, and He's ready to help you change *if* you ask Him . . . so ask Him!

Growing up takes time: Don't expect to be totally wise all at once. After all, if you already knew everything (which, by the way, you don't), why would you need your parents?

WOW

Some people think God does not like to be troubled with our constant asking. But, the way to trouble God is not to ask at all.

D. L. Moody

Waiting patiently . . . for your child to grow up. Some bad habits are simply a sign of youthful immaturity. Expect your children to behave in a manner that is appropriate to their ages, but don't expect perfection from anybody, especially a little child!

Dear Lord,
help me be a person whose
words are pleasing to You.
Help me always to be truthful
and kind so that nothing can
interfere with my love for
others or my love for You.

Amen

Afraid to Tell the Truth?

Remember that I commanded you
to be strong and brave.
So don't be afraid. The Lord your God will
be with you everywhere you go.

❋ ❋ ❋

Joshua 1:9 ICB

Sometimes, we're afraid of what might happen if we tell the truth. And sometimes, instead of doing the courageous thing, we do the unwise thing: we lie.

When we're fearful, we can and should find strength from friends, from family members, *and* from God.

So if you're afraid to tell the truth, don't be! Keep looking until you find the courage to be honest. Then, you'll discover it's not the truth that you should be afraid of; it's those troublesome, pesky lies!

KiD TiP

If you're afraid to be honest . . . ask yourself if you'd rather be *a little* afraid now or *a lot* afraid later.

WOW

Are you fearful? First, bow your head
and pray for God's strength. Then, raise
your head knowing that, together,
you and God can handle whatever
comes your way.

Jim Gallery

Parent TiP

Be courageouly honest in your own dealings with others: you can't teach it if you won't live it.

Dear Lord,
sometimes I am afraid. When I am fearful, let me turn to my family and to You. Then, give me the courage to do the thing that I know is right, and give me the wisdom to trust in You always.

Amen

30

When Other People Lie

People Lie

Do not be misled:
"Bad company corrupts good character."

❉ ❉ ❉

1 Corinthians 15:33 NIV

Sometimes people lie, and sometimes they get away with it. But that doesn't mean that it's wise to lie. And that doesn't make lying the right thing to do. Far from it.

Whatever the problem, lying is always a bad solution. And, besides, lying is always against the will of God. So even if other people lie, don't ever believe that they have *lied successfully*. There's no such thing as a successful lie.

Follow the crowd? It depends! Remember: It's only good to imitate other people when they're doing good things.

WOW

You cannot glorify Christ and practice deception at the same time.

Warren Wiersbe

Follow through in your own commitments and insist that your children do likewise: When you make a promise, keep it. When your children make a commitment, see that they do the same.

Dear Lord,
when I see dishonesty in this
world, let me do my best to
correct it. Let me never remain
silent when I know I should
speak up, because when I am
speaking up for the truth, Lord,
I'm speaking up for You.

Amen

31

Honesty Starts with You!

Those who want to do right more than anything else are happy.

❋ ❋ ❋

Matthew 5:6 ICB

Where does honesty begin? In your own heart and your own head. If you sincerely want to be an honest person, then you must ask God to help you find the courage and the determination to be honest *all* of the time.

Honesty is not a "sometimes" thing. If you intend to be a truthful person, you must make truthfulness a habit that becomes so much a part of you that you don't have to decide whether or not you're going to tell the truth. Instead, you will simply tell the truth because it's the kind of person you are.

Lying is an easy habit to fall into, and a terrible one. So make up your mind that you're going to be an honest person, and then stick to your decision. That's what your parents want you to do, and that's what God wants, too. And since they love you more than you know, trust them. And always tell the truth.

Pray early and often: Have you got questions for God? Anytime can be a good time to pray, even if you must keep your eyes open!

WOW
If we have the true love of God
in our hearts, we will show it in our lives.
We will not have to go up and down the
earth telling everybody about it. We will
show it in everything we say or do.

D. L. Moody

And in conclusion: remember the words of Proverbs 20:7: "The good person who lives an honest life is a blessing to his children" (ICB). Enough said.

Dear Lord,
let me be honest and good,
patient and kind, faithful to
You and loving to others . . .
now and forever.

Amen

Bible Verses to Memorize

Teach me how to live,
O Lord. Lead me along
the path of honesty.

Psalm 27:11 NLT

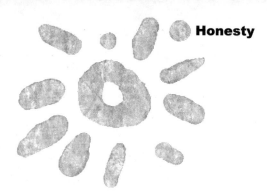

Do to others as you would have them do to you.

✺ ✺ ✺

Luke 6:31 NIV

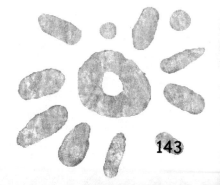

May integrity and honesty
protect me, for I put
my hope in you.

✵ ✵ ✵

Psalm 25:21 NLT

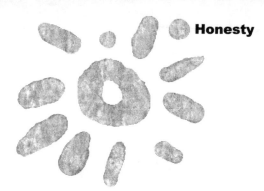

The LORD detests lying lips,
but he delights in men
who are truthful.

✿ ✿ ✿

Proverbs 12:22 NIV

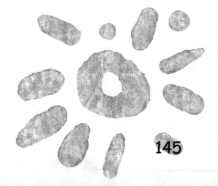

I hold fast my righteousness
and will not let it go.
My heart does not reproach
any of my days.

Job 27:6 NASB

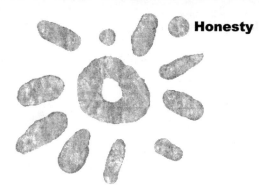

He who walks righteously
and speaks with sincerity . . .
He will dwell on the heights.

✸ ✸ ✸
Isaiah 33:15-16 NASB

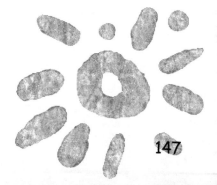

In everything set them an example by doing what is good.

❋ ❋ ❋

Titus 2:7 NIV

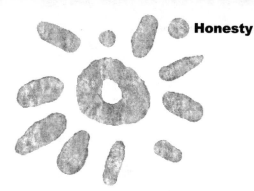

Finally, brethren,
whatever is true,
whatever is honorable,
whatever is right . . .
dwell on these things.

✿ ✿ ✿

Philippians 4:8 NASB

Pray for us:
for we trust we have
a good conscience,
in all things willing
to live honestly.

Hebrews 13:18 KJV

My lips shall not speak wickedness, nor my tongue utter deceit.

✪ ✪ ✪

Job 27:4 KJV

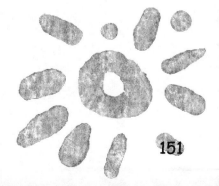

Blessed
are the pure in heart:
for they shall see God.

Matthew 5:8 KJV

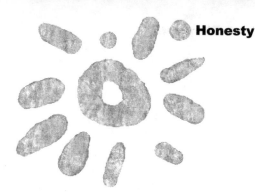

Freely you have received, freely give.

✿ ✿ ✿

Matthew 10:8 NIV

Teach me to do thy will;
for thou art my God:
thy Spirit is good;
lead me into the land
of uprightness.

✵ ✵ ✵

Psalm 143:10 KJV

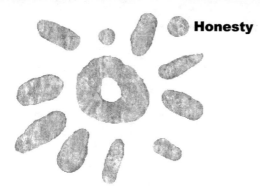

The LORD hates cheating, but he delights in honesty.

❂ ❂ ❂

Proverbs 11:1 NLT

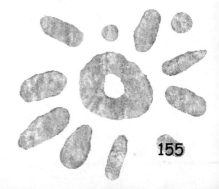

I have set you an example
that you should do
as I have done for you.

✹ ✹ ✹

John 13:15 NIV

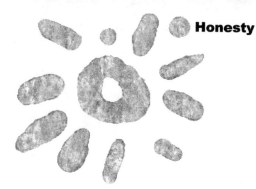

Create in me a clean heart,
O God; and renew
a right spirit within me.

✿ ✿ ✿

Psalm 51:10 KJV

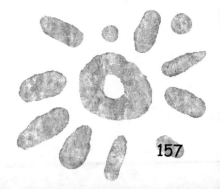

Little Book Devotions help parents and children discuss important Biblical themes by relating those themes to the challenges of everyday life. These books are intended to be read *by* parents *to* children. Current titles include:

Little Book Devotions Honesty
Little Book Devotions Kindness
Little Book Devotions Patience

Additional titles are coming soon.

Little Book Devotions are available in LifeWay Christian Stores.